All about the Music

Julian Thomlinson

D0584520

Series Editor: Rob Waring
Story Editor: Julian Thomlinson
Series Development Editor: Sue Leather

Cengage

Australia • Brazil • Canada • Mexico • Singapore • United Kingdom • United States

Page Turners Reading Library

All about the Music
Julian Thomlinson

Publisher: Andrew Robinson

Executive Editor: Sean Bermingham

Associate Development Editor:
Sarah Tan

Director of Global Marketing:
Ian Martin

Content Project Manager:
Tan Jin Hock

Senior Print Buyer:
Mary Beth Hennebury

Layout Design and Illustrations:
Redbean Design Pte Ltd

Cover Illustration: Eric Foenander

Photo Credits:
44 Photos.com
45 Photos.com

For product information and technology assistance, contact us at **Cengage Customer & Sales Support, 1-800-354-9706 or support.cengage.com.**

For permission to use material from this text or product, submit all requests online at **www.copyright.com**.

Library of Congress Control Number: 2011909969

ISBN-13: 978-1-4240-4646-1
ISBN-10: 1-4240-4646-7

Cengage
200 Pier 4 Boulevard
Boston, MA 02210
USA

Cengage is a leading provider of customized learning solutions with employees residing in nearly 40 different countries and sales in more than 125 countries around the world. Find your local representative at: **www.cengage.com**.

To learn more about Cengage platforms and services, register or access your online learning solution, or purchase materials for your course, visit **www.cengage.com**.

Printed in the United States of America
Print Number: 03   Print Year: 2023

Contents

Background Reading

People in the story

Suki Robinson
Suki is a student at Brenton College. She sings in the band Hometown Alien.

Kurt Linley
Kurt is Suki's boyfriend and the lead guitar player in Hometown Alien. He also studies at Brenton.

Maria Dell
Maria is Suki's college roommate and best friend.

Ash Browning
Ash studies at Brenton and plays bass guitar in Hometown Alien.

Chris Chang
Chris studies at Brenton College and plays the drums in Hometown Alien.

Ben Hamann
Ben is a music company executive.

This story is set in Brenton, a college town in the northwestern United States.

Chapter 1

A surprise for Suki

The message went like this:

"GOT A BIG SURPRISE 4U - U WON'T BELIEVE IT!!!
Tell U Friday. Kurt xx "

Of course, Suki called Kurt right away to find out what it was, but he wouldn't say.

"Wait until Friday," he said over the phone. "I'll meet you in Ben's and tell you then. You'll love it."

Now it was Friday. Suki spent over an hour getting ready. She did her hair and makeup, and put on a new dress she had bought in Seattle the week before. When she went into Ben's Café she was smiling, looking around for him, but Kurt wasn't there yet.

That's OK, she thought, checking her watch. *I'm a little early.* She ordered a coffee, sat down, and thought about Kurt.

Kurt was her boyfriend. They met two years ago, when Kurt was looking for a new singer for his rock band Hometown Alien. He chose Suki. "You sing like an angel," he told her. She never forgot that. Two or three months later they started dating and now, in their last year at Brenton College, they were still together.

Still together, Suki thought. *Are we?* Sometimes it didn't feel like they were. Suki loved singing, and it was great singing in the band with Kurt, but sometimes she wished they could spend more time together, just the two of them.

"Got a big surprise for you," Kurt's message said. She wondered what it was.

This weekend was their second anniversary of being together. Suki was sure the message was something to do with that. Last year they went to Las Vegas together. *What about this year?*

"You won't believe it," the message said.

Kurt walked in about ten minutes later, his long hair down. She stood up and he put his arms around her.

"Miss me?" he said.

"You're late!" Suki replied, trying to be angry.

"I know, I'm sorry," he said, sitting down. "You want another coffee? You look great, by the way. Going somewhere?"

"I've got a date with someone," she replied.

"Wow. Sounds good. Coffee, please," he called to the waiter, then started studying the menu. "I'm hungry. Are you hungry? How was your week?"

"My week was great," she replied. "Now tell me the surprise."

"What surprise?" Kurt asked. He looked surprised.

"Kurt, don't joke around."

"I'm not joking," he said. "What surprise?"

Suki began to read from her phone.

"'Got a big surprise for you,'" she read. "'You won't believe it.'"

"Did I write that?" he asked.

Suki put her phone down. She looked like she didn't understand. "What . . . ? Who wrote it, then?"

Suddenly, Kurt started to laugh.

"Oh, very funny," said Suki.

"I'm sorry." He put the menu down. "OK, here it is. You know Pete who works at The Wheel? He plans all the concerts."

"Yes . . ." said Suki.

"Well, you know that Battle-of-the-Bands competition? The one with bands from all over Washington? The one with the $10,000 first prize?"

"Sure, but . . ."

"We're in it, baby!" Kurt stood up with his arms out. For a moment, Suki didn't speak.

"Are we?" she said.

"We sure are!" he said, taking her hand. "Isn't that great? Do you know how many people from the music business will be there? This is what we've been waiting for!"

Suki didn't quite know what to say. It was good news, after all. No, it was *great* news. So why wasn't she excited?

"Hey," Kurt asked, "is everything OK?"

"Yes, fine. I'm just . . . surprised, I guess."

"You don't seem happy about it," he said.

"Just that it's our anniversary this weekend and I thought, maybe . . ."

"Anniversary?" Kurt said.

"Anniversary, yes. You know, me and you, two years together on Saturday?"

"Yes, yes, of course!" he said, a little red in the face. "Of course it is. I knew that. Maybe we can go for a pizza after band practice? Are you sure you're all right?"

"I'm fine," she said. "Really, I'm fine."

"Good, you know, because I had this idea for a song I wanted to talk to you about . . ."

Chapter 2

Girl talk

It was 10 a.m. on Saturday morning, and Suki was still in bed. Across from her, her roommate Maria was studying. Suki and Maria were best friends, and as best friends, they talked about everything. This morning, they were talking about Kurt. It was a little difficult though, Suki thought, because Maria was having troubles with her boyfriend and didn't seem to like men at all. Suki told her about the night before.

"It doesn't surprise me," Maria said. "Guys are all the same. They never think about anybody else but themselves."

"Maria, that's not really helping," Suki told her.

"I'm just saying," Maria went on. "They always live in their own world, thinking everything they do is important. It isn't."

"The band *is* important!"

"I didn't mean that. Oh, I don't know. I'm just not surprised, that's all."

When Suki came home the night before, she realized she wasn't surprised either. These days, Kurt only wanted to talk about the band. For Suki, the band was important, too, but it wasn't everything. For Kurt, it seemed to be everything. And if the band was everything, what was she? That was the problem.

"It's like this new song," Suki said, "'All about the Music.'"

"What about it?" Maria asked.

"It's a good song. It really is. But there was something about it, something I didn't like. You know what it was? For Kurt, it *is* all about the music. That's all he ever thinks about."

"How does it go?" Maria asked.

Suki sat up straight and started to sing.

> *"It's all about the music,*
>
> *It's all about the song,*
>
> *When your dreams break into pieces*
>
> *And everything goes wrong.*
>
> *Don't worry about tomorrow,*
>
> *Forget about yesterday.*
>
> *Just listen to the music,*
>
> *Let it carry you away."*

Singing the words made Suki want to cry.

"Hey, that's good!" said Maria. "You've got such a beautiful voice. What's wrong?"

"That's not what I mean!" said Suki, crying. "The words—what about the words?"

"It's just a song. Isn't it?"

"Oh, I know it is. It's just . . . Maria, I just feel he doesn't love me anymore."

Maria put down her things and came and sat on Suki's bed.

"Don't get upset, girl. If you really feel that, you need to do something."

"Yeah? Like what?"

"Break up with him," Maria replied.

"Maria!"

"I'm serious. He'll come looking for you, I'm telling you. And if he doesn't, well . . . But he will. Listen. He's a guy. All guys are the same. They're always in their own little world. You need to give Kurt a surprise, get him out of it." Maria looked happy with herself.

"No. No, I can't do that," Suki said.

"I knew you would say that," Maria replied. "How about this, then—leave the band."

"Leave the band?" she asked. "I love the band."

"Maybe if you leave the band AND break up with him, you could see which one upsets him more?"

Maria was laughing. Suki couldn't help herself and started laughing, too.

"Maria, this is serious! Don't laugh!"

"I know. I know it is."

"I'm probably worrying too much. I always worry too much, don't I? Kurt's probably just thinking about this concert. And it is a big thing for the band, really big."

"Hmm, maybe," said Maria. "You do need to relax. I know you love Kurt. And even though all guys are bad, as we know, I'm sure he loves you, too."

"You think?"

"Sure I do. But you're both graduating this year, so he's probably thinking a lot about what he's going to do. Now this competition comes up, and it's a great chance for both of you . . . Hey, I've got an idea."

"What?" Suki asked.

"Why don't you do what he's doing? Just think about the music for a while, see how that goes? You do that, he'll start thinking 'Hey, what's going on? Doesn't Suki love me anymore?' and he'll start running after you."

Suki thought that sounded *a lot* more interesting.

"I like that idea," she said. "I like that idea a lot."

Chapter 3

The anniversary

In Hometown Alien, along with Suki and Kurt, there was Ash Browning on bass guitar and Chris Chang on drums—all of them were students at Brenton College. Chris's dad had a big shoe business, and he let them use one of his buildings for band practice. They went in there about four o'clock on Saturday afternoon to practice for the competition. It was now almost seven and they were still working on Kurt's new song "All about the Music." Suki was wondering when Kurt would say, "OK, let's stop. Suki and I have to go out."

If you're not going to say anything, thought Suki, *then I'm not. You only want to think about the band? Fine. I'll do that, too.*

"OK, let's try that again," said Kurt. "And let's try and get it right. One, two, one, two, three, four."

They started to play the song, but as they got to the chorus, Kurt stopped.

"No, no, no. Something doesn't sound right," Kurt said.

"It sounds good to me," Chris said.

"I don't know," said Ash. "My head stopped working about an hour ago. I need something to eat."

"What do you think, Suki?" Kurt asked her.

Kurt was right, she thought. She had an idea.

"It's C, G, C, F at the moment, right? I think there could be more, I don't know, feeling? What if we change the second C to an A? And then, in the chorus, I could sing the first part low and the second part higher?"

"I'm not sure," Kurt said.

"Can we just try it?" asked Suki.

"Why not?" said Chris.

"All right, Suki," said Kurt. "Let's try it."

They played it. As usual, Ash made a few mistakes, but to Suki at least, it sounded pretty good. Better, anyway.

"What do you think?" she asked them.

"Let's try it again," Kurt said.

They played it again. This time it was better still. The change made a really big difference. When it came to the last chorus, she really put her heart into it, and at the end, she could see the others felt it, too.

"Well?" she said.

"Wow," said Chris Chang.

Suki looked at Kurt.

"It's better," he said. "Well done, Suki. What do you think, Ash?"

"It almost made me forget how much I need to eat," Ash said. "Almost."

Suki felt her face go red. Kurt always wrote the songs, and it felt really good for them all to say that.

"OK," said Kurt. "You know, I think this could be our last song at the concert. What do you think? Hey, why don't we go through it all now?"

"Listen, guys," Ash said, putting down his guitar. "I really, really need to take a break. Why don't we go to Ben's or something, and talk about the songs over some food?"

"Sure," said Chris. "I'm not doing anything this evening. We can leave everything here."

Kurt looked at Suki.

What are you looking at me for, Kurt? Suki thought. *You're not really asking me if I want to have dinner with the guys, are you? On our anniversary, even though it's two years since our first date, and even though last year we went to Vegas together, you don't really want to go for dinner with the band, do you?*

Suki suddenly wasn't feeling so good anymore.

"I don't mind," she said. "We can go if you want to."

"Are you sure? You know, with it being two years and everything."

"What do *you* think?" Suki said.

"Great!" said Kurt. "Hey, we have a table for me and Suki at Cascade, but I'm sure they could take two more. I'll give them a call."

Suki watched Kurt as he took out his phone and called the restaurant.

"Two years?" asked Ash.

"Two years together," said Suki. "It's our anniversary."

"What, today?" said Ash.

"Today."

"Don't you two want to go somewhere on your own?"

"I guess not," Suki replied.

Chapter 4

Together

They talked about the band all Saturday night, and again on Sunday, too. Every night they practiced for the concert. They were playing better than ever, and "All about the Music" was really getting good. But nobody was happy. It all started on the Wednesday when Ash made another one of his mistakes.

"Sorry, boss," Ash said. "I just need something to eat."

Kurt put down his guitar.

"Ash, is that all you ever think about? I mean, could you just maybe, for once in your life, be quiet about eating and think about what you're doing?"

Everyone was shocked. Kurt never spoke like that. But Suki knew why. She knew better than anyone how much Kurt wanted to win the competition, and she knew how tired he was. Still, it was hard to see him acting like this, and Suki didn't quite know what to do about it.

It was now Friday evening, and they were having one last practice before the concert the next day. Kurt was angry with Ash again.

"No, no, no, no, no. A hundred times, no. Your guitar is coming in too late. How many times do I have to tell you about this?"

"Sorry, sorry," said Ash. "Let's try it again."

They tried it again, but this time it wasn't just Ash. Chris was late, too.

"What's going on here?" Kurt said. "Do you understand the competition is tomorrow? Don't you care about this at all?"

Kurt's voice was getting louder.

"Hey, Kurt," said Suki. "Just relax."

"I'm sorry." Kurt replied. "Did you say 'relax'?"

"Yes, relax. Everybody makes mistakes, you too, so let's just get on . . ."

"Suki, can I talk to you outside for a minute?"

"It's raining outside," Suki said.

"Just over here, then," Kurt replied.

They moved to another part of the room. *What now?* Suki asked herself.

"Suki," Kurt began, "please don't make things difficult for me."

"Difficult?"

"It's just not helpful to say things like that. I mean, don't you think we need to stay together on things? It doesn't help if you take the guys' side against me."

"Take the guys' side? What are you talking about?"

"Just that me and you, we're together, so we need to, you know, agree with each other."

"Oh, we're together now, are we? It doesn't feel like it. What about our anniversary last week? Was it just me and you, then? *Together?*"

"Wait a minute. I asked you about that and you said you were fine."

"Who cares what I said? Are you really that stupid? To think I wouldn't care? Do you know how many dates we've been on these last few months? Do you even care about that? Do you even care about me at all?"

Suki found herself putting on her coat. She didn't choose to do it—she just felt it happening. *Am I really doing this?* she thought. It was like watching someone else.

"I don't understand," Kurt said. "Tell me what's wrong."

"What's wrong? *You're* what's wrong. All you care about is the music. You don't care about me."

"How can you say that?"

"Just . . . stop," Suki said, and walked out the door.

Kurt was behind her.

"I have to talk to you."

"I don't want to hear this now, Kurt."

"Please. You have to." He took her hand and led her out of the rain into a shop doorway.

"Suki, I'm sorry. It's true, what you say," he went on. "I can feel it in myself, what it's doing. I don't like it, but . . . I don't know what to do."

She looked up into his eyes. She loved his eyes, and she didn't want to look at them then, but she couldn't help it.

"Suki, I'm not like you. You're really smart, really good at everything you do. The music—it's *all* I can do. I need this . . ."

"It's too much, Kurt. I . . ."

"I need this, and I need you. Can you hear what I'm saying? Without you, there's nothing. There's no band, nothing. I know I've been a bad boyfriend these last few months. I promise, after this competition, I'll make everything right. I really will. Suki, you're everything to me. Come on, just one more day. That's all."

Chapter 5

A thousand people calling your name

Six bands were playing in The Wheel. It was full, almost two thousand people in the main hall. Suki and the others sat backstage, listening to the other bands. Dark Sun was on first. They sounded pretty good, and the crowd cheered when they finished. Next was Antihero. They weren't so good, and the crowd began to boo.

"I feel sick," Suki said when she heard them booing.

Soon Antihero was finished and Pete Chek, The Wheel's manager, came to the door and told them it was time.

"Already?" asked Suki.

Kurt came out first. Ash and Chris followed behind him, then finally Suki, looking at her feet. While the others got ready to play, Suki picked up the microphone and waited. The crowd went quiet, and Suki finally looked up at the sea of people in front of her. The biggest crowd they had before was maybe a hundred and fifty people. It was hard to see because of the lights, but you could *feel* the difference. It was like having a monster in front of you.

A monster that's going to eat you if you sing badly,
she thought.

Suki imagined that she would try to sing, but no sound would come out, like in her dreams. She looked at the others. Ash and Chris looked sick, too. Kurt was checking his guitar like it was just another practice.

Maybe it won't be so bad, Suki thought. Then Kurt started to play, the crowd cheered, and Suki began to sing.

Hometown Alien didn't just play well. They played *great*. There were no mistakes, not even from Ash, and their songs sounded better than ever. When they finished "All about the Music," the crowd went crazy. They were all shouting and cheering. *"Suki! Suki!"* they shouted. Suki couldn't believe it. She felt like she was flying.

There were three other bands after them, but Suki didn't really hear any of them. She hugged and kissed Kurt, and Ash and Chris, too. She saw everyone laughing and talking, but felt like she was somewhere else. A dream, maybe. A new kind of dream. It wasn't until Kurt took her arm, to take her on stage after the other bands finished, that she started to wake up.

Everybody cheered as they walked back on stage. All the bands stood at the back, behind Alanna Gail, a famous singer, and Pete Chek. Suki also noticed some people in suits on the stage—people from music companies, she guessed. Kurt held her hand but his eyes were on Pete, wishing him to say their name.

"We've had a great night of music," Pete Chek said, "and now it's time to find out the winner. Thank you to all the bands for playing, and thanks to all you people for coming out here tonight!"

Everybody cheered again. Pete took a piece of paper and started to thank everyone. A few people in the crowd shouted at him to hurry up. When he finished he gave the microphone to Alanna.

"Come on, come on," Kurt said.

"OK," Alanna said. "In second place, Seattle's own Dark Sun!"

Everybody cheered again. Dark Sun went on the stage and Alanna gave them a check. Suki looked up at Kurt.

"It's us . . ." Kurt said. "It has to be us."

"And this year's winners, and winners of $10,000, as well as a free dinner for four at The Porterhouse restaurant in Seattle, a band who put on a great show for us tonight: White Rabbit!"

Chapter 6

Big music

The crowd cheered again as White Rabbit picked up their prize. Some cameras flashed.

So that's that, Suki thought, then realized she didn't care. The only thing in her mind was that feeling of being on stage, in front of the crowd. That felt like a win to her. She looked at the others. Ash and Chris were OK, but Kurt's face was like someone had died.

"It'll be OK," Suki said to him. "We'll get there."

Kurt didn't reply. Ash came and put his arm around him.

"Never mind," he said. "I'm sorry about the restaurant though—the food there's great."

Kurt looked at him then walked quickly off the stage. The three of them watched him go.

"Maybe you'd better talk to him," Chris said.

Suki guessed Kurt was putting away the instruments, but she decided to give him a moment on his own first. Anyway, she needed the bathroom. She was making her way through the crowd when someone put a hand on her shoulder.

It was one of the people from the music companies, Suki saw, a tall man in an expensive black suit.

"Suki Robinson?" the man said. "I'm Ben Hamann, from Big Music. I really enjoyed your singing tonight."

He took a business card out of his bag and gave it to Suki. Even the business card looked expensive.

"Hi, great," Suki began, not sure what to say. "I mean, thank you."

"No, really," said Ben Hamann. "I thought you guys were the best, for sure."

"Wow. Really? That's great."

"How did it feel? Up there on stage?" Hamann asked her. "You looked like you enjoyed it."

"Yeah. It was just . . . wow. I don't have the words, really. It was . . . like I was on fire, or something."

The man smiled.

"Suki, this may be a surprise, but I'd like to talk to you about a contract."

"A what?"

"A contract. I'd like to offer you a lot of money to make music for us. I'd like to make you a star. How does that sound?"

Suki was too shocked to speak.

"Sounds good, huh?" Hamann said, smiling.

"Yes, I mean, wow, it sounds great, but you really need to speak to Kurt. He's our manager, really, and it's not . . ."

"Sorry, Suki. Maybe I wasn't making myself clear. I wasn't talking about the band. I was talking about you."

"Me?" Suki asked him.

"The band is OK, sure. Good, even. But you're different. You're on a different level. I'm telling you, you could be a star, Suki."

"I don't know what to say."

Suki suddenly felt heavy. Hamann studied her face for a moment.

"You know, most people get really excited when they hear this kind of thing," Hamann said.

"I *am* excited," Suki replied. "Really. It's just that Kurt, our guitarist, well, we're dating, and so . . . He really wants to be a star, too, so he may not . . . you know."

"Yes. That *is* difficult. Look, think about it for the rest of the weekend; give me a call next week, OK?"

"Sure, yes. Thanks."

"Good. But Suki? Be smart about this. And don't take too long. Things like this don't happen every day."

"I know," Suki said. "Thanks."

They shook hands and Hamann disappeared into the crowd.

Wow, Suki thought. *Just . . . wow.*

Then, *What am I going to say to Kurt?*

She was still thinking about this when she turned around to find Kurt standing in front of her.

Chapter 7

Crossroads

"Who was that?" Kurt asked, coming toward her. "Was he one of the music company guys?"

"What, the man?" Suki replied. "He was from Big Music, I think."

"Big Music? What did he want?"

Kurt was suddenly interested. It made it harder to say it, knowing how he'd feel, but at the same time she realized she didn't like the look on his face.

"Oh, I don't know," Suki said. "He gave me his card, and said maybe I could call him. I think maybe he wants to talk about, you know, um, a record deal?"

"Suki, that's great news. Why didn't you let me talk to him?" Kurt asked. "As band manager?"

Suki didn't reply. She looked down at the floor in front of her. *How can I say this?* she thought. But she didn't have to.

"Oh, I see," said Kurt.

"I'm sure it's nothing, really," Suki said. "I'm sure he wasn't serious."

"I see," Kurt said again. "He looked serious to me. What are you going to do?"

"I don't know," Suki said. "I mean, he just asked me. I thought he was talking about us. I didn't know. I mean I told him about us."

"What did you say about us?"

"Just that we were together and that, you know, it may be difficult."

"Difficult. Ha!"

"He just asked me to call him, that was all."

"To talk about a record deal," Kurt said.

"I think so, yes," Suki said.

"You think so, or you know so?"

"I know so . . . I guess."

"Well, that's great," Kurt said, but his face said he didn't think it was great at all. "Two years of hard work, and all for this."

"Even if I do it, it doesn't mean I have to leave the band."

"Come on, Suki. Of course it does." Kurt laughed then. She didn't like the way he said that either. He sounded like a different person. *Or is it me?* she wondered.

"I was wrong about you, Suki," Kurt said. "I didn't think you were only doing this for yourself. I thought it was about us, I really did."

"How can you say that?" Suki shouted. "You're the one who's only had time for the band. You're the one who doesn't want to spend time together. So what? If someone comes along and gives you a contract, you'll say 'oh, no, I can't, I'm in a band'?"

"Yes. That's just what I'd say," Kurt said.

"You're a liar!" Suki shouted.

Kurt's face was cold.

"Let me make this easy for you, Suki. It's over. You. Me. The band. Everything."

He moved past her and started to walk away.

"Kurt, wait," Suki said. But Kurt didn't want to hear any more. He was gone.

Chapter 8

All about the music

Maria found Suki about ten minutes later—the manager let her come backstage. Suki told her what happened.

"Let's get you home," she said.

The two of them went back to their room. Maria made some coffee and they talked late into the night. Suki was upset at first, then angry, and then, after a few hours, she felt calm. She felt changed. The feeling she had on stage, and now this thing with Kurt. It felt like things were happening too fast to do anything about them.

"You can see why Kurt was upset," Maria was saying. "I'm not saying he did the right thing, but I can understand."

Just as she said it, Suki's phone rang—it was Kurt.

"Talk to him," Maria said.

"No," Suki replied, putting down her phone. Kurt called three more times, but Suki didn't reply.

"So is that the end?"

"I don't know," Suki replied. "I just don't want to talk to him now."

They sat quietly for a while. In the end, Maria got up.

"Well, I've got to be up early tomorrow, so . . ."

"Of course. Of course. You've been great, Maria. Good night. And thanks."

"That's OK," Maria said, then stopped at the door.

"Are you going to do it?" Maria asked. "Call this Hamann guy?"

"I don't know," Suki said.

"Sure you will," Maria told her.

After Maria went to bed, Suki sat quietly. She tried to think about Kurt, but kept coming back to that feeling, that amazing feeling she had when she was on stage. She was playing the music again in her head, and it took her a while to realize she could *hear* it. Not just any music either: "All about the Music."

It was coming from outside. She opened the window and looked down to see Kurt sitting in the backyard, playing the song on his guitar.

"Kurt, what are you doing?" she asked him.

"Come down," he replied.

"Kurt . . ."

"Please," he said, and carried on playing.

Suki went out into the yard.

"Kurt, I don't think this is . . ."

"Shh," he said, and began to sing.

"It ain't all about the music

That's where I was wrong

It's just about me and you, babe,

When all is said and done

I love you times a million

More than any words can say

There ain't no music for it

but all I have is yours

and that includes this song

so take it please

and . . . forgive me."

He put down the guitar then.

"Forgive me. Please?" he said.

Suki went over to him, and they put their arms around each other.

"I thought you never sang," she said.

"One time only," he replied.

"Oh, Kurt."

"Suki, I'm sorry. I didn't mean it. I didn't mean any of it. It's great, what happened. It's just, you know. You know how I feel about this. I'm jealous, I can't help it."

"Kurt, you don't have to say this."

"I do. Call this guy. Do it. Whatever you want, I'll be there. If you let me."

"Of course, I'll let you. Are you sure you're OK with this? Because if you're not, I won't do it. I want you to know that."

Kurt shook his head.

"We'll keep going. It's like you said—we'll get there, in the end. And if a big star like you can still play with us now and again . . ."

"Stop it! I'm not a star. I'm not going to be a star."

"Yes, you are," said Kurt, looking into her eyes. "You are. You always were. I knew it from the first time I met you, when you walked into the practice room."

She kissed him for that.

"I know there can't be any promises," Kurt went on. "We don't know what's going to happen, right? But let's try. Can we try?"

"Of course," Suki said, and she meant it. At that moment, she had everything she wanted, and she held Kurt as tightly as she could. But like Kurt, she didn't know what was going to happen. She tried to think about that, but all she could think of was the crowd at The Wheel, calling her name over and over again.

Review

A. Match the characters in the story to their descriptions.

1. _____ Suki Robinson
2. _____ Kurt Linley
3. _____ Maria Dell
4. _____ Ash Browning
5. _____ Chris Chang
6. _____ Ben Hamman
7. _____ Pete Chek

a. bass player in Hometown Alien
b. Suki's roommate and best friend
c. manager of The Wheel nightclub
d. lead guitar player in Hometown Alien
e. singer in Hometown Alien
f. a music company executive
g. drummer in Hometown Alien

B. Read each statement and circle whether it is true (T) or false (F).

1. Kurt forgets their two-year anniversary at first.   T / F
2. Maria thinks Kurt does not really love Suki.   T / F
3. The band usually practices at Chris's house.   T / F
4. Ash and Chris join Kurt and Suki for their anniversary dinner.   T / F
5. Kurt writes a letter to Suki to ask for her forgiveness.   T / F
6. Suki realizes that she loves being on stage and singing.   T / F

C. Complete each sentence with the correct word from the box.

excited	hungry	jealous	nervous
relaxed	shocked	upset	

1. Kurt is very_____ when he tells Suki about the Battle of the Bands competition.

2. Suki is _____ because Kurt does not seem to care about her anymore.

3. Ash always complains that he's _____ during band practice.

4. Suki tells Kurt that he should be more _____ when people make mistakes.

5. Suki feels _____ about performing in front of so many people.

6. Suki is _____ when Ben Hamann tells her that he'll make her a star.

7. Kurt says he felt _____ that Suki was offered a contract, and not the band.

D. Choose the best answer for each question.

1. How did Kurt and Suki meet?
   a. Suki joined Kurt's band.
   b. Maria introduced Suki to Kurt.
   c. They were in the same class in college.
   d. They started talking to each other in Ben's Café.

2. Why does Suki cry when singing "All about the Music"?
   a. She thinks the song is not very good.
   b. She finds the words of the song very beautiful.
   c. She thinks Kurt wants to break up with her.
   d. She feels the song is about her relationship with Kurt.

3. Suki follows Maria's advice to _____.
   a. break up with Kurt
   b. leave the band
   c. break up with Kurt and leave the band
   d. focus on the music instead of Kurt

4. Which band won the Battle of the Bands competition?
   a. Antihero
   b. Dark Sun
   c. White Rabbit
   d. Hometown Alien

5. What happens at the end of the story?
   a. Suki and Kurt break up.
   b. Suki will turn down the record deal.
   c. Suki will accept the record deal.
   d. The band gets a record deal.

E. Complete each sentence with the correct word from the box.

anniversary	contract	chorus	forgive
instrument	manager	stage	upset

1. People perform or play music on a(n) _____.

2. A(n) _____ is the date on which a special event took place in a previous year.

3. A(n) _____ is someone who runs or looks after the band or organization.

4. A(n) _____ is something used to play or produce music, like a guitar or piano.

5. The _____ of a song is the main part that is often repeated.

6. When you sign a(n) _____, you officially agree to work with the person or company.

7. If you _____ someone who has done something bad or wrong, you stop being angry with them.

8. If you are _____ about something, you are sad, worried, or angry about it.

Background Reading:

Spotlight on ... *Famous college bands*

Queen was one of the most famous bands of the 80s. Many of their songs are now classics, like "Bohemian Rhapsody," "We are the Champions," and "We will Rock You." The band started at Imperial College in London, when the lead guitarist Brian May and bassist Tim Staffell took in fellow student Roger Taylor as their drummer. They first called  themselves Smile. Later, singer Freddie Mercury joined and convinced them to change their name to Queen.

Coldplay started when singer Chris Martin and lead guitarist Jonny Buckland met during their first week at University College London. At first they called the band Pectoraiz and later Starfish when Guy Berryman, another student, joined. After the last member Will Champion joined, they were forced to change their name to Coldplay, because another band had the same name!

Creed is an American rock band that was popular in the late 1990s and early 2000s. They had hits like "My Sacrifice" and "One Last Breath." Lead singer Scott Stapp and guitarist Mark Tremonti met in high school but formed the band when they were students at Florida State University in the United States. Brian Marshall and Scott Phillips joined the band soon after, and they released their first album three years later, in 1997.

Think About It

1. Do you know any more famous bands that started in college?

2. Have you ever taken part in a band competition? How did it feel?

Spotlight on . . .

Getting a recording contract

Here are five great tips to get that record deal you deserve.

1. You need a demo CD. A "demo" is a recording made in a studio of your best songs. Recording companies listen to many CDs every day, so they will probably listen only to the beginning of each song. Make sure they are good!

2. Call the recording company and ask who you should send your demo CD to. Make sure the package is addressed to that person.

3. Perform at local competitions. These are great places to show everyone how good your band is. Talent scouts (people looking to sign contracts with good bands) go to these shows.

4. Build your name. Create a band website or join Facebook or other social media websites. Make some T-shirts. Put up posters and give away flyers. Perform for free. Let people know who you are. You may want to put your songs on the website for free or give away CDs of your music at concerts so people can share them with others.

5. Practice, practice, practice. You never know when the right person comes to watch you play. Make sure all your concerts are good. You can play anywhere and anytime—on the streets, at your school—anywhere there's a crowd of people.

Good luck!

Think About It

1. Which piece of advice do you think is the most important? Why?

2. Do you know of any artists who were discovered on the Internet?

Glossary

anniversary	(*n.*)	An anniversary is the date on which a special event took place in a previous year, e.g., a wedding.
contract	(*n.*)	A business contract is an agreement between two people or companies to do something.
cheer	(*v.*)	When people cheer at a concert they make a loud noise of approval.
chorus	(*n.*)	The chorus is the main part of a song and is repeated.
competition	(*n.*)	A competition happens when two or more bands try to be the best so they can win a prize.
crowd	(*n.*)	The large number of people watching a concert are the crowd.
forgive	(*v.*)	When you forgive someone for doing something bad to you, you tell him or her it's okay.
graduate	(*v.*)	When you graduate from college, you leave it and start working.
instrument	(*n.*)	Pianos, guitars, and drums are musical instruments.
record deal	(*n.*)	A record deal is an agreement to make songs and sell them.
stage	(*n.*)	The stage is the place where people play music in a concert hall.
upset	(*adj.*)	If you are upset about something, you are sad, worried, or angry about it.